Encounter The Divine

By Rochelle Rossey

Book Cover Design by: SelfPubBookCovers.com/RL Sather

Acknowledgement

After reading many books about angelic beings, my angels and their purpose in my life have been defined to me. I have read and heard many true encounter stories about people being pushed out of harm's way by invisible hands, angel's appearing in human form to assist people in times of desperation, and I have even read about angel's voices giving emergency instructions in the nick of time to avoid disaster.

Our angels guide us during our earthly life and communicate with us in ways we do not realize. God has commissioned them by our side to be our everlasting companions and caretakers. The greater a person's belief in angels, the more easily a person will recognize their divine assistance. It is believed that children are more receptive to visions of these beautiful beings.

I remember sitting in church one Sunday and witnessing an unusual display from a little girl who was being held from her father in front of me. She pointed ahead of her and shouted excitedly, "Angel - big angel!" I gazed toward where the little girl was pointing and I did not see any statues or portraits of angels that would explain this reaction from a child. At that very moment I knew that this young soul was given a glimpse of something heavenly that would be lost in her memory as time passed.

Since holy angels derive their power from God, our lives are an open book of possibilities. By choosing to acknowledge their assistance and guidance, doors will open to a more fruitful life. Angels yearn to be near to us. It is through them that we may draw nearer to the living God - not only in heaven, but within us as well.

Divine guidance is available to all of us if we desire to become receptive to it. Messages from our angels can reach us in the form of lyrics from songs, words of wisdom from strangers or friends, or written words from publications.

This book was written twenty years ago and sat on a shelf collecting dust until I recently decided that it needed shared with others. Although most of the angel stories were contributed by family and friends, a few of these experiences were written by the individuals who experienced them. I want to thank my friends from the Pittsburgh area who shared their personal life experiences with me for this book in the hopes that their stories would inspire others.

I hope that at some point during the reading of this book your spirit will feel a sense of excitement; as if you are being awakened from a deadened state of existence to a new state of life. Happiness comes easier once the secrets of inner peace and spiritual self-growth are realized. We all seek inspiration to carry us through our doldrum existence. Inspiration ignites our spirits and allows us to experience moments of awe and revelation.

After years of inspiring lessons and miraculous events I have learned that - YES there is a GOD. YES, there is a heavenly realm invisibly surrounding us, and YES there are angels and spirits assisting us every day, every hour. In fact, an angel may have inspired you to choose this book for enlightenment and growth. It is believed that our life experiences create spiritual lessons that are necessary to impart new wisdom and integrity upon our soul.

We are all beings made of spirit and flesh. Our spirit is always striving to connect to our universal God, and our flesh is always striving for earthly satisfaction. Our conscience is our only connection to what is true to our inner being. When guilt tends to surface from our actions, we become aware that we are out of synchronization with our spirit, and synchronization of our physical mind and spirit is the key to true contentment and happiness.

Enlightenment of the spirit is a gift of wisdom and knowledge imparted upon us by the Heavenly Father. It is a spiritual understanding of what is true and just. When we become enlightened, we become one with God, the universe and the spiritual realm around us. Once awakened to God's power and love, you will be lead spiritually to greater "heights" of understanding. New truths will come your way. Your neighbors, acquaintances and friends who you once may have viewed as failures or losers - will now be viewed on a soul level. You will see them as a spirit walking on a different life path learning different life lessons than you.

Books pertaining to spiritual growth will pop out at you from the book shelves at libraries or bookstores. Inspiring people will cross your path. You will happen upon television programs with hidden messages, but you will no longer miss the messages, you will understand them!

Section 1

True Angel Encounters

The Basement Stairs

Contributed by Shawn Bezak

I've always had the highest respect, love and trust in
our Lord, Jesus Christ. He had always helped and
comforted me on countless occasions through many health
problems and feelings of despair.

My family and I will always give him thanks for the
miracle of life. At the age of six I underwent a serious
open heart surgery to repair three holes in my heart. I
pulled through with a 50/50 chance of making it.

During the time prior to surgery as a little child, I
never felt sick and was always happy. I never realized until
I was older that I had a serious problem. I was guarded
most of my life with great love and care from my parents
and two sisters.

At the age of 23 I fell in love with a young man
who was very kind, loving and always striving to better
himself in life. We married six years later. Heaven came
down to earth for me the day we exchanged vows before
God, and with His grace our love has remained strong for
many years.

But one night my heart became burdened with depression. My husband and I attended a concert in Pittsburgh. Although we were out together with friends on this particular night I felt alone and sad. Lately, I had been experiencing bouts of depression because I felt as if my husband was devoting too much time to his business and friends. As I sat there at the concert my mind was convinced that my husband didn't love me anymore.

We stopped at a local bar on our way home and while there I began to accuse my husband of ignoring me and acting as if I wasn't a part of his life anymore. I ended up leaving the bar and walking home to our house a few blocks away.

While at home I worked myself up into an angry frenzy. Without thinking I grabbed an armful of dirty clothes and headed down my old, rickety basement stairs to do laundry. Suddenly, I had a most unusual flashback. I envisioned an old friend of mine. She had died years earlier from falling down a flight of stairs. Before I knew what had happened, my sock got stuck on a nail at the top of the wooden stairs. I lost my balance and couldn't grab onto the walls because my arms were full of clothes. I called out, "Jesus save me" and closed my eyes to whatever was to happen.

I felt myself falling head first down the steep stairs toward the concrete floor below. As I was heading down the steps, I felt as if I was moving in slow motion. I must have blacked out because I have no memory of falling after that point. When I opened my eyes, I found myself laying on my side on the cold basement floor.

I slowly got up and inspected myself. I didn't have any visible cuts or bruises. I then looked toward the steps and I couldn't believe it. I immediately knew that something miraculous had happened. I was about four feet away from the bottom of the last step, and had somehow avoided hitting into the concrete wall that jutted out at the right of the bottom of the stairs. Since our home was built over 80 years prior, our basement walls were made out of large uneven boulder-like stones that could cause injury if a person hit into them.

I truly believe that I had some heavenly assistance that fateful night. I feel that I was saved from injury to help me realize that my earthly time is precious with those who love me. If I ever experience feelings of insecurity, I try not to let it get the best of me. I remember that October night and am reminded about how much I am loved and cared for.

The Brush of a Wing

Contributed by Rochelle Rossey

During my teenage years a group of friends and I traveled to the New Jersey shore for a summer vacation. While visiting a crowded beach for an afternoon 'suntan session' the four of us were forced to place our beach blankets at the very edge of the beach near some grassy knolls due to the large volume of people visiting that day.

While I was laying on my back soaking up the sun, a fly or insect kept landing on my leg. I was getting irritated and had to keep swooshing it away with my hand. This kept up for a few minutes until the insect planted itself on my leg. It wouldn't budge when my hand attempted to swish it away time after time, so I quickly sat up to see what it was. Suddenly, a long metal pole fell on my beach blanket from a shed behind me. It was being used to secure a set of doors shut on a small shed.

The pole was not real thick and resembled aluminum. I didn't think twice about the incident until I rose to move it. In trying to do so, I couldn't budge it! The pole was extremely heavy. I couldn't move it without the aid of two of my friends. Suddenly, I realized that it had fallen exactly where my head was positioned and goose bumps immediately crept over my upper body.

Who knows, maybe the object landing on my thigh wasn't an insect after all, but the brush of an angel's wing!

Spirit Guidance

Contributed by Robert A. Bellus

A number of years ago I was in a business partnership with a gentleman who professed not to believe in the spirit world. Late one afternoon we decided to go for a ride in his new pick-up truck to grab some lunch. As we approached his vehicle to return home, my friend couldn't locate his truck keys. Looking inside the vehicle, he saw the keys still hanging in the ignition where he had previously left them.

We had a few miles to drive and my friend didn't know what to do about the predicament. He didn't want to damage a window in his new vehicle and he didn't desire to walk the half mile to a public telephone. (Neither of us owned a cell phone back then).

I thought that a few private words to whatever power(s) may happen to be around might be helpful. *'Oh please, dear creatures who may hear my thoughts, please open his truck's door.'* Almost instantly both door lock buttons sprang up and the doors became unlocked.

My business partner couldn't grasp the miracle and with a breath of relief exclaimed, "Well, I guess our eyes weren't seeing right." Being a believer in spiritual beings, I knew otherwise.

Strength From Above

Contributed by Pastor Robert A. Pollick

At a fairly young age I was blessed with the gift of
pastoring a church in Clarion, Pennsylvania. While
running the ministry and guiding the congregation, I also
had the job of guiding and caring for my wife and three
young children.

One day I decided to spend a day with the children
and take them for a ride in our '62 Buick. While out on the
road one of the front tires became flat. I pulled the car off
the road and parked it up against a metal fence. I permitted
the children to get out, but warned them, "Please don't go
near the front of the car." Although the car was in its 'park'
position, I knew there wasn't much room between the car
and the fence and I didn't want the kids in front of the
vehicle while I was jacking up the car to change the tire.

Shortly after replacing the tire, the jack gave way
and the car lurched forward. I heard a scream. I looked
and saw my five year old son, Jeffrey, pinned between the
car and the fence. I immediately panicked because the
weight of the car was crushing him. My children and I ran

13

to his rescue and attempted to squeeze ourselves between the car and the fence to push the heavy vehicle away from his body. Our efforts were in vain - we couldn't budge the car.

When my son collapsed, my heart was pulled from my chest. I thought I had lost him. In desperation I prayed. "Please God, help me." I then tried again to push the car away from the fence and suddenly the car lurched high up into the air and flew straight back about five feet! I couldn't fathom how that happened, but I had no time to think about it. I grabbed my unconscious son from the ground, flung him in the car and drove him to a nearby hospital. When I arrived there, he awoke. After a series of x-rays it was confirmed that nothing was broken and he had escaped injury.

I've learned at an early age that you have to go by faith to God, and God and his angels came on the scene for me that day.

Pushed to Safety

Contributed by James Haitz

I've crossed many streets in my lifetime without incident, but one day, many years ago an incident opened my eyes to the unexplained. I was eight years old at the time and decided to walk down town. As I reached the bottom of the hill at First Street in Wilmerding, I stopped to observe the one way traffic. When traffic looked clear, I began to slowly jog to the other side of the road; as was my usual practice back then. While in the middle of the street I realized that traffic wasn't clear after all for a car happened to suddenly appear. Since the sidewalk was a distance away, I flung myself with arms extended outward to safety.

I then immediately felt a force push me from behind and I seemed to actually fly to the sidewalk and into a clump of bushes. I remember seeing the car speed past me; missing me by inches.

As I climbed out of the bushes I remember wondering who had pushed me to safety. Whoever it was seemed awful strong and powerful. But I couldn't see anyone on either side of the sidewalk. I was in a daze and just surmised that I was a very lucky boy.

As I reflect upon this experience as an adult, I realize that I was evidently saved from injury or death for some reason or another. Only God knows.

Through the Clouds

Contributed by Kathleen Monzo

While traveling with my sister-in-law and my two young children from Pittsburgh to the suburbs of town, I encountered a rare glimpse of angelic intervention.

My sister-in-law, Cindy, was driving her Bronco truck in the fast lane of traffic and was just about to merge into the slow lane before entering a tunnel up ahead. As a force of habit, I glanced in the passenger side mirror to make sure traffic was clear. As soon as I spotted a tractor trailer truck looming up beside us, I yelled, "A truck is coming!"

Cindy jerked the steering wheel sharply to the left causing the Bronco to lose control and spin. It then felt as if the truck was picked up off the ground and I saw white clouds surrounding us. Time seemed suspended as we spun in and out of the lanes of traffic. Before we knew it, we were on the other side of the tunnel and didn't know how we had gotten there.

17

I turned to Cindy and asked, "How did you do that without hitting any cars?" She answered, "I don't know, I had my eyes shut the whole time."

Since my mother was deceased, we both immediately felt that she had somehow interceded for our welfare and offered her daughter and grandchildren some heavenly aid.

Back Seat Angel

Contributed by Donna Latimer

My mother passed away when I was seven years old. Although I deeply missed her physical presence over the years, I always felt her spiritual presence watching over me as I grew into adulthood. Difficult situations always seemed to work themselves out although they seemed impossible at the time.

One day while in my early twenties I was sitting at a red light waiting impatiently for it to turn green. Since I was an impatient driver, my foot was positioned to hurriedly push the gas pedal down to the floor as soon as I was able. As the light turned green, I was just about to drive ahead when a voice yelled out from my back seat. It shouted something very loud, but I didn't know what it said. I immediately became frightened and glanced behind me thinking that someone had made their way into my vehicle, but I found an empty back seat. Just then a large coal truck barreled through the intersection in front of me at a fast rate of speed.

19

I knew then that I would have been hit by the heavy truck if I would have driven ahead immediately after the light had changed. I was shaken by this revelation and pulled over into a gas station to inspect my car further. I even went as far as opening my trunk to make sure there wasn't a person hiding inside it.

Although I went through the motions in trying to locate the source of the 'loud voice', I knew in my heart that something unexplainable had happened. Something that saved my life.

While preparing this story a dramatic realization came to mind. My mother died in a car accident while in her twenties. She preceded through a green light and was struck broadside by a vehicle that ran a red light. I could have been killed in the same manner if I wouldn't have been distracted that fateful day. Whether the voice I heard was from an angel or my mother - it guided me safely home to my newlywed husband.

He Spoke Through a Child

Contributed by Rosemarie Haitz

During the early years of my motherhood I spent much of my leisure time visiting my large family. My children had many cousins to play with while the adults mingled and visited with each other.

One day my husband and I took our children to my cousin's farm for a picnic gathering. We were all sitting outside watching the children play when a cloud burst suddenly appeared. I helped usher the children into the house out of the rain and the screen door was locked behind us. The adults gathered in the kitchen area to eat and the large group of children were ushered into the adjoining room. We were having a good time laughing and sharing stories when my cousin's eleven year old daughter walked into the kitchen and asked, "Can we go swimming?"

The surrounding adults seemed oblivious to the girl's question and kept on socializing. The girl's mother told her daughter that the pond was too deep and muddy for swimming. But, the girls question struck a mysterious cord in me. 'Swimming?' I whispered to myself. The dammed-up pond in my cousin's backyard came to mind. I rose from my chair and hurried to the screen door. Just as I peered out, I saw my 18 month old son, Jimmy outside walking gingerly on a cement wall above the pond. He was at the highest point on the wall, which was about six feet high. I knew if I yelled to him he may become startled and would either suffer an injury falling into the yard or he could fall into the deep pond below him.

I ran out onto the porch and started running up the hill of the backyard. Within seconds Jimmy lost his balance and fell into the pond. I panicked. I didn't even think of calling for help, I just needed to get my son out of the murky water. I jumped into the five foot pond and began to frantically scoop up water with both arms. It was difficult to feel the bottom of the pond with my hands since the water reached my upper chest, and the dark water made it impossible to see anything below the surface.

It seemed an eternity before I scooped my son up in my arms. It was while holding him high above my head that I began to scream for my husband. Upon seeing me holding the child, he and a few relatives hurried to climb the steep grassy hill to assist me. I remember seeing him and the others struggle to make it up the hill since the grass was slippery with mud. I didn't remember having any issues getting up the muddy hill when I was hurrying to save my son; in fact I didn't even remember any mud.

I feel that God spoke to my heart that day through a child. I was meant to hear the girl's question and that question saved my son's life.

The Face of Pure Love

Contributed by Mary Wilson

In the seventh year of my marriage I began to experience depression. I was unhappy with my spouse and unhappy with my life. Although I prayed to God often about my dilemma and continued to remain a faithful Catholic, I couldn't seem to shake the feeling of doom that came over me at times. I felt that there may be no way out of my unhappy situation unless I divorced my husband, and that realization played havoc on my mind.

One day I sought alcohol to relieve my depression. After a few drinks my mother called me and asked me to pick her up at work. After arriving at her office she noticed my drunken state and informed me that she would drive us both back to her house.

While at my mother's house I continued to drink. My mother was very concerned about me and protested against it, but I didn't listen. We were both sitting on her back porch listening to music when I stood up on a wobbly chair to dance to a song on the radio. Suddenly, I lost my balance and began to plummet backwards over the balcony of her 15 foot high porch.

Almost instantly a blonde haired man appeared on my left side and grabbed me. He had the bluest eyes I had ever seen and was wearing a white robe. He looked past me and said, "Don't look to the right." I don't remember anything from that point on except opening my eyes and briefly seeing my mother above me telling me that help was on its way. I didn't realize it at the time or remember, but I was airlifted to the hospital in a helicopter.

I awoke in the emergency room and saw the same man wearing blue scrubs. He was holding my wrist taking my pulse. Then suddenly he was gone. My body felt sore but I didn't feel any pain. I asked the nurses where the doctor had disappeared to and they said that there was no doctor on staff that fit this man's description. I was told how fortunate I was because I had only sustained bruises - no cuts or broken bones in my fall.

After this experience I had no doubt about the presence of guardian angels. I even decided to name my angel. The name 'Raphael' immediately came to my mind. It was a name I was not familiar with, but felt it was a good name for my angel. Suddenly I began to come across the unusual name everywhere. I would see it in books and printed objects. I also learned that Raphael meant, 'God Heals Us' in Latin.

Well, God not only healed my depressed heart, he healed my marriage and I feel as if this experience has changed my life forever. I will never forget my angel's beautiful face and how he touched my heart. I now view everything in a spiritual way instead of a worldly way. I also believe that although I may not feel Raphael's presence, he is always there guiding me and keeping me safe from physical harm and injury.

The Protector

Contributed by Robert A. Bellus

An elderly lady related to me a somewhat unusual experience she had encountered many years ago. The woman resided five miles from where she was employed near the city of Pittsburgh. She was asked to work late one night, and when she left her office it was well after ten o-clock.

She had problems for whatever reason getting a taxi, so she was forced to walk home. She shuddered when she realized that she must walk through a very tough area that late at night herself. Since she had no choice, she said a quick prayer for protection and began on her way. After walking about two miles she saw a brute of a man walking toward her. The woman told me, "My heart started to beat a mile a minute in knowing I was about to be mugged, robbed or possibly worse. There was nobody else on the street so if I screamed, who would hear me?"

The man stopped when he was five feet in front of her and blocked the sidewalk so she could not move ahead. Suddenly out of nowhere, a huge German Shepherd dog appeared by her side with fangs bared and a powerful growl coming from its throat. The would-be assailant quickly stepped off the sidewalk and crossed the street leaving the woman alone with the animal. The dog walked along the woman's side the whole way home. When she reached her premises, she went inside to bring him some food. When she returned, the dog had vanished.

Cross of Protection

Contributed by Carolyn Barrack

There is one childhood memory that has remained in the recesses of my mind. The memory of a friend whose life ended at the age of thirteen. When I learned that she had been electrocuted by lightning during a storm at camp, I was devastated. I had just spoken to Rita earlier that morning as she sat beside me at Sunday School. What had bothered me the most about her death was that she was burned beyond recognition. Her pink shoes were the only evidence left behind; the same shoes she wore that morning.

The incident instilled in me a fear of lightning and storms. Over the past forty years I have often put myself in Rita's place imagining the horrible, painful death she must have experienced all alone on the beach. Her death at such a young age has affected me most of my life.

One night while standing outside Victory Chapel, a homeless shelter where I worked as a volunteer, a storm began to develop. Nancy, a resident of the shelter was standing directly in front of me on the sidewalk. She

mentioned that she had to make a telephone call. Just then
I noticed a flash of lightning in the sky. I said, "You better
get inside it's starting to lightning, but I wouldn't use the
phone yet."

Nancy took my advice. Moments later she stepped
from my path and headed toward the side entrance door of
the Chapel. Suddenly, we heard a loud booming noise and
saw a long white streak of light barreling down from the
sky toward us. I screamed, "Oh, Jesus!"

Moments later I examined myself. Although I saw
the bolt of lightning directly in front of me, I didn't feel any
pain or sensation of being hit. When I found that the gold
cross hanging around my neck was indented on one side
and charred black, I was stunned. It was evident that the
lightning had struck my cross, but God had spared my life
and the life of Nancy who had just moved away from the
path of the lightning. Nancy, myself and another woman
who was in close range of the lightning truly felt blessed to
be alive.

After this incident the cross fell off my chain on two
occasions. Since it was a gift of love from a friend and
bore special meaning to me, I felt it best not to wear it in
case it would fall off again and I would lose it.

One day a few weeks later, I felt an urging to place the necklace around my neck again. Soon after the most unbelievable thing happened. While standing outside the shelter with two other residents of Victory Chapel, another bolt of lightning fell from the sky and landed between myself and another woman.

This was totally unbelievable. How could this happen to the same person twice within a short span of time? After much contemplation and thought about these incidents, a new truth and realization hit me. Aside from feeling blessed to have survived the ordeal, I no longer felt that my childhood friend had suffered as I had imagined she had for all those years. Her death was instant - as quick as the bolt of lightning that had hit my cross.

Also, I noticed a difference in my attitude about storms and lightning. I was no longer afraid. Twice within a month's time, I could have been killed by lightning, but God protected me. I guess he felt I needed to take notice so he placed two miraculous incidents in my path (literally) to awaken me and heal me of my unwarranted fear and worry. My trust in God has increased and my life will be forever changed by my cross of protection.

The Yellow Birds

Contributed by Edward Emerson

While growing up in the suburbs of Pittsburgh, I spent a lot of time at a nearby fishing hole. In the summer I would fish at the secluded pond, and in the winter I would play ice hockey there with my friends.

At the age of fourteen my two friends and I ended up at the fishing hole on a snowy January afternoon. We began clearing off the snow that was covering the pond so we could play ice hockey. After clearing the snow we noticed something unusual. A cluster of bright, yellow birds, similar to canaries, appeared on a single branch that hung out over the pond. They began acting hysterical by squawking and flying off and on the branch they were sitting on. Their brightness stood out amid the white snow around them and the loud noises they were making seemed uncanny in the dead quiet of winter. Then just as suddenly as they had appeared, they flew away.

Immediately after their departure my friends and I heard a loud pop then a cracking noise. We realized the ice was beginning to crack around us. We hurried and ran from the middle of the pond to safety. As we reached the edge of the pond, water had already begun to engulf the area we had just left. We counted ourselves real lucky after we realized we could have been killed. The pond was located near an abandoned farm, there was no one around to assist us if the need would have arisen.

I believe the birds were divinely sent to warn us about impending danger. If they wouldn't have distracted us, we may have been too caught up in our hockey game or scattered about the pond in different directions instead of pausing to watch them, and someone may have slipped beneath the cracking ice.

I Know I Have Cancer

Contributed by Janice Roskey

Many years ago in the middle of the night, I was aroused from a deep sleep by a loud ringing sound, similar to a bell. Upon awakening, I immediately heard a voice inside by head. "You have cancer," it conveyed. Of course at first I did not heed the warning because I felt I may have been dreaming.

One month passed and late at night I was once again awakened to a ringing sound and the same voice stating, "You have cancer." The next day I scheduled an appointment to have five moles removed, all were benign.

Over Easter break, my aunt a nurse anesthesiologist, sat across from me at dinner. Pointing to my neck, she warned. "Your thyroid doesn't look right ... you need to have that checked."

A family doctor ran a series of thyroid tests, and all were negative. But the late night warnings grew more emphatic and the voice now stated, "You have cancer in your throat."

It was then that I decided to heed my aunt's suggestion and consult a specialist.

Soon after I visited an endocrinologist. When I walked into his office he looked at me, pointed to the chair and ordered, "Sit down, you have a tumor on your thyroid." After the aspiration and a follow-up x-ray, a complete thyroidectomy was performed. The tumor was malignant. I did, indeed have cancer! I was informed by the doctor that the tumor was very large and it had been growing for years. If I had not sought his advice the tumor could have been fatal.

I am forever grateful to the divine guidance that saved my life and has kept the cancer away to this day. I often wonder why the voice didn't return stating, I told you so.

Section 2

Spirit Communication

Spiritual Communication

Whenever someone we love leaves this world, we are plagued with questions, "Are they really with God?," "Are they happy?," "What are they doing in Heaven?." We cannot imagine our loved ones living a life in spirit form away from us. This is where the difficulty of accepting death occurs. One part of us wants to believe in Heaven, but we can only hope in its existence.

I have met and spoken to many people who have experienced communication from loved ones who have passed on - myself included. I have also met those who have had a supernatural experience from the invisible realm that surrounds us.

Animals are tuned into this realm that we cannot see and infant babies as well. They have the ability to see angels and spirits that we cannot see. Until of course the baby grows and this ability is lost in its earthly memory.

This section is about spirits who have reached out to their loved ones from beyond to assist them in accepting their deaths or to give them hope or courage when needed. As strange as this may sound, death is to be the most wonderful experience of our life! The joy a spirit experiences as they step into the heavenly realm cannot be explained. Not only are spirits in the company of those they have loved who have passed before them, but they are still able to visit their loved ones on earth and assist them by inspiring their thoughts when necessary. They are around us when we need them to be or ask them to be, whether we feel them or not. And, most importantly, their love for us never dies. They do not miss their earthly life or suffer in any way possible - it is the family left behind who suffers.

My reasoning for sharing the following stories with you is to prove that LOVE EXTENDS BEYOND DEATH. Miracles do happen and can happen to assist us spiritually along our life's journey. Thousands upon thousands of people in the world have witnessed communication from beyond, but few feel comfortable enough to speak of this communication to others.

A friend of mine shared a story he had heard from his neighbor who had lost her husband. In her younger years while she and her husband were married they had vacationed in Holland and purchased a pair of wooden shoes as a souvenir. As their children grew, so did their love for the wooden shoes. They would take turns wearing them around the house. Needless to say, the loud noise the shoes made while being worn on bare flooring became unnerving and her husband hid them away from the kids up in their attic.

The shoes were still in the attic some twenty or so years later when the woman's husband died. While coming home from the funeral she proceeded to walk up the stairs to her second floor. To her amazement she found the wooden shoes sitting on the top landing of the stairs side by side. Since she was the only other person who knew where the shoes were hidden, she was sure it had been her deceased husband who placed them there to let her know that even though he was gone physically, he was still there for her.

Heaven is not some faraway place on the other side of the universe, it is invisibly around us. I have learned from personal experience that our loved ones do still care about us from the other side and their only desire is that we move on with life and not be crippled by their departure and absence.

Being a clairvoyant person I have been able to communicate with spirits on the other side. I can't explain how I am able to do readings or why I was given the ability to do so, but I do know that deceased loved ones care most about us moving on with our life after their departure and desire for us to be successful and happy. They also want their families to know that they are in a state of contentment and peace in another realm.

I would like to share the following story I have written about my mother's death and how I was blessed with a miracle after she left our world.

Miracles from Mom

The area surrounding my mother's hospital bed was void of character. The mechanical contraptions in the intensive care unit added to the gloomy atmosphere.

I stood beside my mother's bed holding her hand tightly. My husband and I, along with my two sisters and father, were waiting for the bouncing green line on the monitor behind my mom's bed to flatten. We were waiting for mom to leave us forever. A drawn curtain was the only separation between my family and the nurse's station.

A tear formed in the outside corner of my mother's right eye and I wiped it away for her. I was worried that she was sad to have to leave us and was crying out from within. She knew that I was due to have my second baby any day now, and her other daughter's were going through emotional times as well. My younger sister was getting married in two months and my older sister was going through a divorce.

As I stood beside mom's bed, pain began to shoot through my swollen, pregnant stomach and I sat down in a chair beside the bed. I was trying to ignore the dull aches all evening, but the pain became increasingly worse.

Soon after, the green line flattened on the monitor and the horrible flat lining sound echoed throughout the room. A nurse solemnly drew back the curtain to disconnect the machine. I wobbled from my chair and hurried beside my mom to say goodbye. Between tears I told her that I loved her and asked her to watch over us from Heaven.

Afterward while sitting in the waiting area my contractions began to occur three minutes apart. I was numb with grief and unable to cope with the realization that I may actually be in labor. *Not now,* I thought. *Not tonight.* When a nurse heard about my predicament, she insisted that I call my doctor immediately. I remember walking back into the intensive care unit to use the telephone at the nurse's station. (Since this was thirty years ago, I didn't have a cell phone). My mother's body was lying nearby behind the drawn curtain awaiting pick-up from our funeral director.

After my doctor heard the disturbing news about my mother he ordered me to get to Magee Woman's Hospital in

Pittsburgh immediately. So my husband and I left one hospital to travel to another at the opposite side of town. It was already after 11:00 p.m. and I was drained physically and mentally.

After being admitted to the hospital I learned what I had already suspected - I was in labor. I wasn't mentally or emotionally ready to concentrate on the endeavor ahead. My mother wouldn't be here to assist me or participate in the happy celebration as she was for my first baby's birth a year and a half ago.

The hospital staff were very comforting to me during the labor process. One nurse sat beside my bed a good part of the evening speaking at great lengths. She kept my mind busy and helped me focus on the situation.

Early the next morning I was wheeled into the delivery room. I remember calling out mentally for my mother. The pain was so intense. I wanted relief, I wanted my mom! As I was preparing to give birth, I envisioned my mother looking down at me from above the delivery room. I felt her presence and love very strongly in an unexplainable manner. I felt connected to her. I knew then that she was there to witness her granddaughter, Alyssa's birth.

That evening I awoke in my hospital bed in the middle of the night. It was around 3:00 a.m. My room was pitch dark except for light filtering through the crack of my bedroom door. I instantly remembered my mother's death and the darkness suddenly disturbed me.

I got out of bed and turned on the light. I then saw a chair sitting directly beside my bed. It was so close that it was touching the side of the mattress. This chair was on the opposite side of my bed stand against the back wall of my room before I went to sleep that previous night and I had no visitors who would have moved it. Again the feeling of my mother's presence occurred. I felt that her spirit was in my room and had visited me to give me strength throughout the night.

Although I was blessed to have felt these feelings, months passed and I began to question the validity of them. Maybe I was just imagining these feelings because I yearned for that closeness with my mother once again. I also still had doubts that my mom was happy in Heaven.

Being Catholic I decided to pray a novena to St. Therese of the Little Flower. I prayed for a miracle to give me faith in knowing that my mother was truly with God. I specifically prayed for my mother's rosary beads (which I now possessed) to turn from silver to gold. I had heard that this miracle was occurring throughout the United States and I felt that maybe God could bless me with this miracle to confirm my faith; even though it was a lot to ask of him.

A few days after completing the novena my maternal grandmother died. While at the funeral home I approached my grandmother's casket with my cousin to pay my respects. As we stood together praying, I noticed something. The silver links of the rosary beads entwined in my grandmother's right hand had turned a bright yellow color similar to gold. I had just removed these beads from my grandma's dresser drawer a few days earlier to give them to the funeral director and they were not gold at that time. The links were silver as are most rosary beads. I knew then that my prayer request had been answered, but in a manner that would surely get my attention. I also knew that the tear my mother had shed on her deathbed was a tear of joy - not sorrow. And, who knows maybe my mom met my baby girl as they passed each other through Heaven's portal.

Don't Be Afraid

Contributed by Cindy Brutout

Some of my fondest childhood memories were of my Hungarian grandmother. Her love of baking and hand stitching doll clothes was only a small portion of memories I can easily recollect. Her big heart and loving manner toward me was the most endearing part of her character. I adored her and she made me feel special to be a part of her life.

Since my parents both worked, my grandmother took on the responsibility of sending me off to school and caring for me. Because of this she spent many nights at our house.

Although I was only seven years old when my grandmother died, I was grief stricken. Where did she go? Was she really in Heaven? Would I die next? Would she come to get me since she loved me so much? These questions haunted me as my family visited her home often after her death.

While staying overnight at her house I couldn't sleep as these questions invaded my mind. Death was all I

45

could think about as I lay in bed listening to traffic zooming by on Route 66.

Suddenly my grandmother appeared at the foot of my bed. Although the room was completely dark at the time, there was a light glow surrounding her. She was wearing a pink nightgown, and her long hair was pulled up in a bun as it usually was. She calmly said, "Don't be afraid, Cindy." After this message she faded out and disappeared. Although I was frightened upon seeing my grandmother, for some reason I was then able to sleep.

As I look back at this incident many years later, I now realize that my grandmother only wanted to help strengthen me during this difficult time. She came not only to calm me, but to help me realize that she is still there for me, but in a different capacity.

Mom's Heavenly Advice

Contributed by Linda Vucelich

Much to my dissatisfaction, my mother and I always had a strained relationship. Being the only offspring and female compounded the difficulty of our relationship. No season of my life as a young girl or as an adolescent or a woman into adulthood could improve our connection; instead it worsened. My mother began to exhibit severe behavioral patterns which left me feeling smothered, manipulated, overprotected and unloved.

All I wanted was a normal, healthy mother/daughter relationship. Instead, our relationship gave me exhaustion, no peace and an intensifying amount of anguish until her death.

Two weeks prior to my mother's death my family learned the nature of her fierce behaviors. It was an all-encompassing illness that affected the brain structure and manifested itself in the emotional, mental, social, physiological, neurological and psychological dysfunctioning of her person.

This diagnosis provided the missing piece of the puzzle and helped to explain forty-two years of my life and gave the reason she was not able to be supportive or present for me in the capacity I so desired. A transformation began in my life with this awareness.

I recognized on a personal level that my mom's illness provided me with an excuse to avoid dealing with what I needed to do on a professional level. I realized that it would be necessary and imperative to take a course of action for change, except my vision was limited and my feelings of frustration clouded the issue. My attitude also necessitated a radical adjustment. I did not know what course of action to take to accomplish my goals and guidance was needed.

After my mother's death, my father had given me the small amount of money accrued from my mother's insurance policy. He had a sense that she wanted me to have the money even though my father was the beneficiary. This sum remained in my savings account as my anguish about my future mounted.

Three months after my mother's death I received guidance in the middle of the night. I was awakened by a voice calling my name. I immediately recognized the voice, it was my mother.

I would imagine fear and/or doubt to be the first normal reaction one may experience in a case such as this. However, I felt no fear as my mother began to give me specific instructions on how and when to proceed toward resolution of my situation and frustrated feelings. My deceased mom's voice said, "Divide the money you were given and it will give you time. Begin in September and take one week vacation from work to rest. Then present the idea to your employer to take one day off every week from work . Utilize the insurance money to compensate for the loss in pay. There will be no loss of money and you will gain time to make other monies. First, use the time and energy to organize yourself and your home. Next, begin to expand and seek fulfillment elsewhere with your skills and talents. Events will come to assist you and things will happen. Give yourself the time with the money you now have. In this manner, the attitude will change on its own. Enjoy, be fulfilled and create."

This information was crystal clear and left no room for doubt. I became peaceful and accepted the words as a gift from my mother. Although her physical death eased the stress I had lived with for years, her voice yet lived to deliver a message from beyond the grave that she was not able to communicate while living.

I felt it was an act of her love for me. This communication provided me with another transformation. I felt guided, supported and loved. Previous negative feelings towards my mother were replaced with compassion and understanding.

I followed her directions accurately. Her guidance led me to unimagined territory and personal fulfillment was a result of my t'ai chi instruction and interest in health. A path began to open. My attitude improved. My love for my mom opened and I received, although in a different manner, my long-held wish for a mother/daughter relationship.

God Had Other Plans

Contributed by Cathy Conrad

My mother died after a long battle of Legionnaires Disease and complications from Lupus. Nothing more could be done for her and I convinced my father to let her go. She was very tired from her battle and for the last two weeks of her life she had been placed on a morphine drip and feeding tubes. All her major organs began to malfunction and I deeply felt that she wanted to go home; not to our home, but home with God.

One of the hardest realities the family had to face was that our mother was leaving us at the young age of 59. I knew I wasn't ready for her to die. I wanted her to see my children grow and to be there for all those special occasions that fill our lives. My mother and I were just starting a friendship and we were beginning to understand each other as adults. But, this must not have been in the master plan and prayer helped me realize that no matter what I wanted, God had other plans.

It was a few weeks after the funeral and I had gone to bed with a mind full of thoughts. I awoke with a start -

someone had been calling my name very softly. I looked around the bedroom and there sitting on my travel trunk was my mother. She was dressed in her daily attire of jeans and a flannel shirt. She had a serene look about her and when I tried to speak, she placed her fingers to her mouth as if to say, "Shhhhh."

I noticed I wasn't upset or frightened at seeing her, instead I felt a peaceful feeling come over me. This could have been because my mother looked so peaceful herself. All the pain I had remembered from the hospital had disappeared from her face. After a few moments, she vanished. I feel that my mother's appearance to me was her way of saying, "I'm okay."

Since her death I have buried my favorite uncle and my father. Neither have come to me as she has, but when I feel stressed, unsure, or experience something that I feel they would have enjoyed, I feel their presence and then all is okay.

Life is short and precious. We need to be reminded that although circumstances may not turn out the way we desire them to, it's because God had other plans.

Martha

Contributed by Julie McNamara

I had just gotten home after a long day and flopped backwards on my bed. I was exhausted and felt sleep quickly overcome me. Just as I was almost asleep, I heard my name being called three or four times. As it aroused me, I recognized the familiar voice immediately. The voice belonged to Martha, a long-time friend of my mother. I didn't think to question how she could speak to me when she was not physically in my room, I just proceeded to answer, "What?" with my eyes still tightly closed.

Martha began to give me a message, not an internal message, but an audible one. She informed me that I must have my mother contact her because she was slipping away in a coma and needed to see my mother before leaving. She asked, "Do you understand my message?" I replied, "Yes" and agreed to pass the message on to my mother. I then feel into the deepest sleep imaginable.

The next morning I told my mother what had happened and asked her to please give her friend a call. When I returned home from work that day, I asked my mother about Martha. The shocked look on her face told me that she had forgotten to call. I couldn't understand how this could have happened, but she quickly reached for the telephone and began dialing. My mother asked if Martha was available and she was informed by her daughter that Martha was taken to the hospital early that morning. Martha had been asking about my mother until 2:30 a.m. when she slipped into a coma. The daughter had no way of contacting my mother since she misplaced her address and telephone number.

After getting all the hospital information, my mother hung up and began to pack for her long journey to see her friend. As she was packing, I began to wash dishes and peered out the window in front of me at the beautiful day. It was then that I saw an unusual sight. In the distance I noticed a white object on a green hillside against a blue sky. I also saw writing below the scene and could make out Martha's full name. There was additional lettering below her name, but I couldn't read it. I told my mother what I had seen and told her to pack extra clothes and take flowers because I felt strongly that this would be Martha's last day.

My mother called me from the hospital later that day to tell me that she arrived in time to see Martha.

Although she was still in a coma she squeezed my mother's hand before passing away.

When my mother got home she handed me something that she said I'd recognize. It was the memorial card from Martha's funeral. A white dove flying high over a hillside with a blue sky. Below was Martha's name and date of death. The exact vision I had seen a few days before. My mother thanked me and left the room.

If Martha's spirit would not have communicated to me when she had, the reunion between herself and my mother would not have occurred. It would have been more difficult for my mother had she not seen her good friend before she died. Martha's spirit realized that a reunion was necessary for both of them. Sometimes good-byes release the spirit and assists it so that it can contently continue on whatever path awaits them.

Streetlight

Contributed by Edward Emerson

One summer while in my early teens I experienced a supernatural phenomenon that has significantly affected me throughout my life. I had joined some friends to play a pick-up game of football, and as evening drew near I lost track of time, or at least that was the excuse that came to mind. Having been warned on several occasions to be home before dark and realizing it was after 9:00 p.m., I headed for home.

I decided to take the long way home on my bicycle to avoid the short-cut through the Lutheran Cemetery which was just down the street from my home. As one might imagine, riding a bicycle through a cemetery at night would constitute unusual behavior, to say the least.

The Lutheran Cemetery was one of two cemeteries side-by-side separated by a line of over-grown locust trees. Some of the graves dated back to the early 1800's and several had pictures of the deceased on small porcelain plaques, which I found to be slightly unnerving.

As I peddled the long way home, the reality of being late started sinking in and I began to pedal faster. As I rounded the bend past the first cemetery, I began to hear what sounded to be someone singing church hymns. At first an "Alleluia" could be heard and as I peddled on more words became clear, but I can't recall them now. Just as I approached the locust trees which separated the two cemeteries, the streetlight above me suddenly went out. For reasons I do not know, I stopped in the darkness. Standing no more than ten or fifteen feet in front of me in the middle of the road stood the source of the church hymns I had heard.

A spiritual being dressed in an all-white robe stood where busy traffic normally drove. Its hood was up over its head and its hands were covered with long sleeves. The bottom of its robe hovered above the ground covering its feet. I could see a thick white rope tied around the waist. Each end of the rope had a large knot with frayed ends.

I could clearly see the pale face in the darkness. No features stood out to me except little black, button eyes. I could not tell if this person or presence was male or female, but I noticed a soft glow surrounding it. I do not recall feeling afraid or threatened or wanting to peddle away, I just stared at this presence for at least a minute, maybe less, when suddenly the hymn ended mid-verse.

"Do you love your parents?" the being asked.

I responded, "Yes."

"Do you believe in Jesus Christ?"

Once again, I responded with a "yes."

"God bless you," or something very close to that were the final words spoken to me. During this time no cars passed by, which was unusual for such a busy street and the streetlight remained off.

Suddenly, this presence began to sing the same hymn, picking up where it had left off. The next thing I recall, I was peddling my bike and looking behind my shoulder.

As I peddled away, I saw the being fade away around the bend behind me into the darkness. At that very instant, the streetlight turned on and a car passed me on the road. I do not remember peddling my bike past this spirit or it passing me, I only remember looking behind me and watching it fade into darkness around the bend, which was probably a distance of 150 feet or so. It was as if time stood still for some duration.

I rode my bike home and ran into the house. There at the kitchen table playing cards was my mother, sister and aunt. I looked at them and then at the clock. When I saw that it was almost 9:30 p.m., I was surprised. Even taking the long way home should have only taken ten minutes at the most.

"Would you care to join us?" my mom asked with no mention of being late. I then told my family what had happened to me, but they did not offer any opinions or explanations as to this strange occurrence.

Being an adopted child, I felt it odd to be asked if I had loved my parents by the floating manifestation, but perhaps I had the rare opportunity to meet my guardian angel or a heavenly spirit willing to manifest itself to me for purposes beyond my knowledge.

Over 30 years have passed since this experience and its affect still remains with me. I am now married with an adult child and to this day when I am driving too fast or there's an accident or a deer up ahead of me or I'm having a less-than-perfect thought, the streetlight in front of me goes out as if to warn me, or more importantly, to remind me of that evening in my youth.

A Conversation With Dad

Contributed by Janice Roskey

My dad died from lung cancer and his death was slow and arduous. Unlike many deaths, we had time to discuss our thoughts and we planned his burial. We also made peace with many issues which occurred during my 43 years as his daughter.

About six months after his death I was aroused from a deep sleep. My father chose to awaken me to talk! I found it a bit unsettling and crazy that he and I were conversing extensively about numerous items at three a.m., however, my portion of the dialogue was not the spoken word, it was simply thoughts. He, in turn, would answer my questions patiently, but not actually in his voice as I remembered it.

During his life, my father drank extensively and suffered from depression. He assured me these behaviors were part of a larger plan. For about an hour he explained that we all choose our parents and all of us have lessons to learn. People we encounter, many times, were with us in previous lifetimes. Another voice chimed in, and I believe it was his brother who preceded him in death. I rarely saw my father happy during his life, but this encounter was extremely positive.

Toward the end of the conversation I stressed to my dad that I really needed a sign that I wasn't going crazy, that this wasn't merely a dream and that I wasn't merely talking to myself. He gave me the sign I needed. He also joked that most people want a lottery number.

"Your front door is unlocked," he boasted.

"No, it isn't. Dad, you know how paranoid I am about locking my doors."

I lived alone and have had numerous bad experiences, thus, I exercise extreme caution. He then called me my pet name, which assured me it was indeed my dad. "Pretty face … go look. Then will you believe me?" he asked.

I stomped down stairs to find the front door jamb unlocked. My friend had entered my home that evening through the front door and exited through the garage. I then had forgotten to lock the main entrance. I haven't heard from my dad since. Maybe I need to leave the door open again.

Section 3

Our Purpose and

Mission

Our Purpose and Mission

Besides gaining knowledge and wisdom throughout our life experiences, we are sent to earth for a special purpose or to fulfill a predestined mission. Whether our purpose is to give birth to a child that will contribute much to society, or whether our mission is to learn how to love and forgive, we are all born to make a universal difference. Even though we may be meant to spend only one day on earth, we affect those who come into contact with us. We influence our families, co-workers, friends, friends of friends, etc. The list goes on and on. Our presence is felt by many. Every person who is involved in our life serves some sort of purpose in our spiritual development. Whether it be a brief relationship or friendship there is a reason for them to be in our life.

I once heard about a woman who had a horrible relationship with her mother-in-law. After the mother-in-law passed away she appeared to her one night. She first apologized to her daughter-in-law for her treatment of her during her lifetime, but then stated, "Through me you learned tolerance and patience."

In the movie, <u>Simon Birch</u>, young Simon feels early on in life that he is to play an important role in some way and that his birth defect (dwarfism) occurred for a reason.

Simon ends up rescuing some classmates on a sinking school bus and catches pneumonia which leads to his death. If Simon wouldn't have been so small, he wouldn't have fit through the bus window to save his friends. So, his dwarfism did play a major role in his life purpose.

We all have a purpose or many purposes. I have watched many television shows about people trying to communicate with loved ones on the other side. I was moved when I saw the story about a woman who had lost her one year old baby daughter. She wanted to know why she was taken so young. The mother was very emotional and upset while relaying her story to a medium who was present to assist communicating with her daughter. The mother was told that her child's purpose was to experience love in her short lifetime, and although she was very young when she passed, the love she experienced from her parents was intensely felt by her. Thus, her mission or learning experience was completed. If this is truly the case, it proves that emotions can be felt on a soul level - not a human level.

It is difficult to spiritually rationalize the death of an infant or child, but although that infant or child was taken from this world prematurely, it still had a purpose to fulfill and sometimes it is in their death that this purpose comes to

light. Every incident happens for a universal reason. I
don't want to say that good things always develop from a
tragedy because I find that hard to believe while people's
hearts are ripped apart in agony. But, I will say that in
tragedy - new life is possible for those affected.

I read an article about a local teenager who was
diagnosed with bone cancer. In the article he stated that if
it wasn't for his cancer he wouldn't have met so many great
people. So, through his illness he was able to see some
'good' that uplifted his spirit.

There was a time in my life when I had come to
know two women who had suffered the loss of a child.
Through their courage they chose to share their stories with
me in the hopes that others may be inspired. Although their
children's spirits did not stay with their families on earth for
long, their presence affected many around them and in their
community.

Silence is Golden

When Linda and her husband learned that their
newborn daughter, Katherine, was dying -- no words of
comfort could help ease their pain. Two weeks before her
due date, Linda noticed a difference in the baby's activity

and movement. After seeing her obstetrician it was learned that the baby's heart rate was three times faster than normal and a cesarean section was immediately scheduled.

Shortly after the birth, Katherine's vital signs began to fall and she began to experience seizures. The Texan doctors were dumbfounded about her condition and had no explanation as the medical reasoning behind her failing health. The next day it was verified that she was 'brain dead'.

Being devoted Catholics, Linda and her husband desired to have a priest anoint and bless their daughter. But in Texas that alone was a task since there was a major shortage of Catholic priests. They were relieved when a priest was found, but when he appeared to perform the short ceremony the smell of alcohol was overbearing and his unstable movements were beyond belief.

For some unexplained reason, Linda and her husband chose to silence themselves about his intoxicated state, and the next day the life support system was disconnected and Katherine died peacefully in her mother's arms.

Linda later received a letter from the priest who baptized Katherine. Although he didn't apologize for his actions, it was evident that Katherine's death had affected him. He wrote, "I honestly believe that I have a personal angel now to pray with." This letter assisted Linda's family in their healing. For although her daughter was only on earth for four short days, she managed to influence a wayward priest who needed spiritual guidance. Katherine's wisdom was beyond our understanding.

Jason's Act of Love

When I first met Nancy I couldn't believe that this small, petite woman had experienced such a terrible tragedy. This woman came to visit me to share a tragic story about her infant son. Even though the events occurred over twenty years ago, they will still have a huge impact on anyone who reads her story.

Nancy and her husband were on their way home from a party one evening when a vehicle ran a stop sign and slammed into the side of their van. The impact hit the driver's side where Nancy was sitting. She was eight and a half months pregnant. Nancy sustained life-threatening injuries. Her diaphragm was lacerated and both of her legs were broken. She remained in a coma for days after the accident. Her baby boy, Jason, was born dead with a lacerated liver and spleen. Nancy's husband also sustained injuries that kept him hospitalized, but the injuries were not life-threatening. For days Nancy's children and other family members didn't know if she would live through the ordeal.

Upon gaining consciousness Nancy had learned that her baby had died, and nothing could prepare her for the long road of depression that lay ahead. The family also learned that the man who hit them that night was drunk. Lawyers informed the family that homicide charges could not be pressed against the drunk driver because of the law in Pennsylvania. In Pennsylvania at the time of the writing of this story, *'a viable person was one that took a breath.'* It was decided legally that Jason was not a viable person because he did not take his first breath.

The family began their long, legal battle to change this law. A friend of Nancy's wrote a poem about Jason and it was sent to the Governor of Pennsylvania along with information about the crash.

Nancy and her husband were eventually contacted by the Governor's office and a meeting was set up for them to visit with him. During this meeting they were asked permission to distribute their poem to Congress the next time the house was asked to vote on this Bill. They were granted permission and later learned that the law had been

68

changed in their favor because of their actions. But the change would not affect the rulings in their particular case since the law came into effect after their vehicle accident.

After meeting with Nancy I learned an unusual fact concerning the accident. If she would not have been pregnant, the impact would have killed her. As difficult as this is to imagine, little Jason cushioned his mother's body and prevented her death that night. So, although her unborn son was not able to share his life with his mother, he shared his love in a manner only he and God could understand.

The following is a copy of the poem that was distributed to Congress many years ago. In Jason's death, victims will now be able to experience justice in the state of Pennsylvania if a similar situation should happen to occur in their lives.

Were You Thinking About Me?

While I was growing day by day, my mother was getting sick ... that's when she started thinking about me.

She told my father ... was he surprised!
That's when he started thinking about me.

They told my brother and my sister ... they were so excited
to hear that they would have a baby brother or sister to love
... that's when they started thinking about me.

Then my mom called all the family and all of her friends ...
that's when they started thinking about me.

Our doctor listened to my heart and took care of mommy
... that's when he started thinking of me.

The lady who did my first sonogram saw my tiny hands
and feet ... that's when she started thinking about me.

I kicked my sister right where mommy put her hand ...
She was really thinking about me.

My grandmas, aunts, and mommy's friends had a big party
just for me ...they were so happy.
Mommy announced my name that day ... "Jason Russell"
They were all thinking about me.

We were riding home in the car that same night ... I felt
safe and warm...
then another car hit us and I went to be with Jesus ...

He has always been thinking about me.

The doctors and nurses took me out of mommy's belly … it was too late … that's when they started thinking about me.

The policemen arrested the man who hit us …
That's when he started thinking about me.

All the people came to see me at the funeral home…
They were all so sad while they were thinking about me.

Now my mommy is in the hospital with lots and lots of pain … she will always be thinking of me.

How about you? Are you thinking about me?

You say that I was not a person because I hadn't taken at least one breath … well, I would have, in fact, I could have, but I didn't get the chance.

I have only one question … While you were making up this law … were you thinking about me?

In loving memory of Jason … June 29, 1997

Section 4

Tips to Motivate Your Spirit

Tips to Motivate Your Spirit

It's so important to make our daily agenda a happy one. One day while driving to the high school track for a brisk walk, I noticed the hustle bustle of the early morning throughout my neighborhood. I saw two men concreting a driveway, I saw workers pounding shingles in place on the roof of a house, I drove past a Federal Express truck and I saw the mailman making his rounds. It seemed as if they were all just following daily routines like robots. As if they didn't have any control over their life or future.

The following motivational tips were written to open a pathway and assist the reader in finding other ways to deal with circumstances that may upset them. By dealing with life on a soul level instead of a human level, life can be less stressful and fulfilling.

In order to develop spiritually we need 'food for thought' or 'words of wisdom' to open up our mind to inspiration and motivation. We need to really think about what we desire to FEEL in life, not what we desire to POSSESS.

If you are living a doldrum life - day after day - you will lack vitality and energy. You will notice that it takes a lot to get your day going and to keep it going. Balance your life and create the environment you dream about.

Open your heart to renewal and rededication to the temple you possess within. The temple that God designed.

Never Say "If" Say "When"

All of us were born with divine gifts. It could be the gift of singing, writing, counseling or just being a good listener. Whatever the gift is that we possess, we must use it actively or we will feel dormant in our life. Our creator helped us along by laying the groundwork in our talents, but it is up to us to develop these abilities and creative gifts.

We will never reach full contentment unless our heart is in tune with our soul. In other words, we are following our hearts desires. I often hear the remark, "If only I would have done this or if only I would have done that ..." An _"If only"_ attitude drains our spirit. If a person puts off desires or accomplishments, their life will only just BE, and we are bigger than ourselves.

Whatever your gift - develop it - nurture it. It will soon become an entity to you. It's also important to not let negative remarks from others affect your judgment or desire to follow the path you feel inclined to.

While pursuing my writing career, I used to hear comments such as, "There's no future in it" or "There's too much competition to make it successful " from family and friends. But the comment that crushed me the most was from a very close loved one. He said, "It's a pipe dream - it will never happen!"

I then explained to the person making that comment that I will never say "IF," I will always say, "WHEN" I get published." Because in my heart - by doubting that success would ever occur in the first place from my divine gift, would be doubting God.

If you have no idea what your gift or talent is think back to your childhood and remember what you enjoyed doing most back then. Sometimes we have talents and interests as children that our soul really enjoys, but these interests become stifled in adulthood.

I remember writing song lyrics and poetry at the age of eleven. Writing was in my soul way back then, but I placed it on the back burner and forgot about it. It was only after rejuvenating my love of writing as an adult that I felt complete and excited again about my life.

Be true to yourself and search your soul for inspiration and direction in your life. Use your divine gift as often as possible - it replenishes your heart and spirit. It's important to remember that inspired thoughts come from Heaven. How can we fail if we are listening or following the voices of God and his angels?

Forgiving is the Mirror to Our Soul

For some people it's a difficult task to forgive because the word "pride" acts as a barrier. It's much easier to be upset rather than to just let things go. I've heard of families that have silenced themselves against one another for years before excusing the past hurts of others. How can this behavior ease the resentment they feel toward the avoided party? I can only see it making the situation worse and more difficult to deal with.

Forgiving others will lift your spirit to a new realm of understanding and wisdom. Peace and contentment will be experienced. God desires us to be *All Forgiving* and when we act against this, we can easily be denied peace of mind in our life. Just ask yourself, "What is the worst thing that can happen to me if I forgive a person that has wronged me?" I'm sure you won't even know how to answer this. But, I can assure you that your spirit will be greatly affected in a positive way.

I realize that some people have hurt others in terrible ways, but to be able to come face to face with that person and say, "I forgive you," is a great turning point in a person's life spiritually and emotionally; it's a humbling experience.

Over the years I have met some interesting people. But, I'll never forget a particular woman I met while attending a college course in a neighboring community. She had been a victim of physical abuse at the hands of her father and she shared some insight with me about the terrible ordeal she had experienced over and over again as a young child. She told me that she was always filled with anger and resentment toward her father until she decided to confront him as an adult and express her feelings and emotions about how the events affected her life. After doing so, a long overdue healing process began.

She learned that alcohol and blackouts were part of her father's life while he was inflicting pain upon her. But since her father was clean for years now she decided to share her emotions. Well, needless to say, they both ended up going to counseling together and began the process of moving forward with healing and now have a wonderful relationship; as hard as that is to believe.

I have learned over and over again that a person cannot be content for long if they harbor feelings of hate and animosity toward another person. Living life without resentment is the key to good emotional health.

As a young child I experienced sexual abuse. I have written the following story describing my pain and emotional turmoil in the hopes of healing others who may have been unfortunate enough to have experienced a similar situation.

Face the Music or the Tune Will Never Stop
An Incest Victim's Opinion

It was Father's Day and every greeting card I read was inappropriate, "You are the best Father," - "Thank you for all the special memories." I didn't know what I was looking for, but I was sure I wasn't going to find any card that read, "Thanks for ruining my life!"

When I was eight years old my father fondled me and touched me inappropriately. After these few horrible occurrences, I became fearful in my own home. I began to act out every time my mother decided to go shopping or leave the house. I remember clinging to her legs, begging her to stay or to take me with her. I hated the idea of being left behind with Dad because I never knew if it was going to happen again. Fortunately, there was never another episode - at least not to my knowledge or memory.

For the next fifteen years or so I lived in a "pretend" world, keeping this secret hidden from friends and family and acting as if nothing had ever happened to make my world fall apart.

79

While in my early twenties, I began to awake in the middle of the night to find my father sitting at the bottom of my bed. The old feelings of nausea returned, and I would move my legs and act as if I was awakening to remove him from my room. This was a very uncomfortable experience, which I feel has contributed to me being a light sleeper.

It was around this time that I decided to break the silence and share my story with my two sisters. In doing so, I learned that my older sister had been a victim for years at the hands of our father. My youngest sister was not molested. I feel that her heart condition may have fended Dad off. She was born with three holes in her heart and had open heart surgery when she was six. I feel that he probably didn't want to chance triggering a health crisis with her, so he avoided her altogether.

But suddenly I began to understand my older sister's rebellious nature toward Dad. After sharing our stories with each other, we kept on pretending while we lived at home with both parents. Since Dad was a decorated Army veteran who served his country for 28 years in both the Korean and Vietnam Wars, many people throughout our community thought the world of him so I just "pretended" that he was only a war hero.

Many more years passed and in 1989 our mother died at the age of 59. To our knowledge she never knew about the abuse.

After mom's death I decided to confront my father. I will never forget that day - it's etched in my mind; just like the days of my abuse. I sat beside him at the kitchen table and said, "Dad, Tammy* and I remember what you did to us and we think you need to talk to someone."

Silence. Total silence. He stared at me blankly and asked, "What did I do to you?"

I realized then that he was not going to confess to his actions. Although my heart was hoping for that, it wasn't going to happen. I then explicitly explained what he had done to me and handed him a telephone number of a sexual disorder clinic in Pittsburgh. He didn't admit to his actions at that time, but said that my mother wasn't interested in pleasing him sexually and it left him frustrated. My only comment to him was, "Oh, so you turned to your children!"

After leaving his home that evening, I felt such a flood of relief. The burden was somehow lighter to carry now and I felt empowered that I confronted him. Although

*Name changed

this confrontation occurred over 20 years ago and my father has since passed, I feel as if I was healed from 'pretending' any more. One thing I have learned about secrets is that they can drain the life out of you. I mean, let's be real. If you bury something long enough, it will ROT!!

Over the years I had to also seek counseling since I inherited characteristics of victims of sexual abuse. I was co-dependent, self-abusive, distrustful of everyone, and fearful. Both my sister and I experienced with drugs while growing up and we could never say NO to men who wanted some physical attention. Although my mind would cry out NO - I didn't feel as if I was allowed to speak my mind with the opposite sex. I didn't feel it years ago, and I didn't feel it most of my adult life.

Pretending for many years set a pattern of behavior in me. It had become much easier to just PRETEND everything was okay instead of voicing my opinion. I have seen this behavior take hold of me in my troubled marriage where I ignored problems for years to avoid feeling uncomfortable or dealing with confrontation; which I hated.

After my dad's death, I found a photograph of him taken in Vietnam during the War. On the back of the photo in my dad's handwriting was a short story - it read:

On top of Ankhe Pass in the Central Highlands
between Bridge 17 & 18 QL19 day of ambush in the pass.
We ambushed the ambushers and wiped them out. It was a
classic situation. We waited until they were on top of us
and engaged them in hand to hand combat before they
realized we were there. None of them escaped. Two
Koreans killed and I had one man wounded. The Tigers
called me the white winged warrior because of my white
hair and deadly attack.

I can't explain to you how I felt after reading this
passage from my father, but my feelings toward him shifted
a little after this point. My first reaction was one of shock.
My dad was always a very quiet reserved individual and
spent much time reading and painting. Although he
mistreated myself and my sister, I just couldn't imagine him
acting with deadly force toward another human being. And
then as strange as this is to say, I immediately developed a
sense of pride toward my dad. He fought as a combat
soldier should have fought for his country. And, who
knows maybe serving in the Korean and Vietnam War

screwed him up somehow and affected his personality; maybe it caused him to be the way he became.

And if there is any truth that we choose our parents, spouses, children, etc. to learn spiritual lessons then maybe my dad chose to be a catalyst. Maybe he was meant to act badly toward us to aid us in growing on a soul level because I definitely learned how to FORGIVE a person who did a great injustice toward me.

I know that sounds very strange to think that abuse can ever be a good thing in any sense - but I do remember talking to my local priest about the molestation and he said, "Because of the adversity you experienced you have become the person you are today."

Who really knows, but it gets you thinking - doesn't it??

Revitalize Yourself

Many of us find ourselves rushing every minute of each day. We rush to work, we rush to meet deadlines, we rush to pick our children up. This lifestyle can overcome us and we find ourselves rushing when there is absolutely no need to.

One day my six year old daughter was giving me a difficult time at bedtime. I began to get impatient with her since it was a school night and insisted that she get to sleep. I eventually worked myself up and could see that it was affecting my daughter. After realizing this, I calmed down and something came over me. As I quietly tucked her back in bed for the tenth time - I looked into her sweet face. I saw my daughter in a different light. Instead of seeing an uncooperative child who was causing me grief, I saw a child who desired her mother's love at bedtime.

Sometimes - SLOWING DOWN makes a person view situations in a different light. Taking time each day to be quiet and alone with our thoughts is essential to our well being. Whether it be relaxing in a hot tub of water, meditating, or taking a walk, quiet time nourishes us and renews our spirit. We all need to receive direction from God in our everyday decisions and it is only during quiet moments with ourselves spent reflecting that God speaks to our hearts and minds.

I feel that God and his angels are always trying to communicate with us, but we are never quiet enough to hear their divine guidance. Instead of blasting the radio while driving to my destinations, I now choose to LISTEN and RECEIVE guidance. Inspirational thoughts and ideas easily formulate during these times and I find many answers to my problems.

We Should Be As Children

By possessing the simple traits of children our life can become more exciting and happy. When God stated, "We should be as children" he desired for us to imitate their innocent characteristics. For instance, children never need to put forth effort in being happy. Joy seems to come naturally to them (unlike adults). They amuse themselves with the simplest of toys and games, and their friendliness is overwhelming. They are always readily anxious to play with others whether they know them or not. There is rarely an adjustment period needed when meeting with new playmates. For adults it's a chore to mingle with people they don't know. In fact, most of us dread attending functions without the presence of acquaintances or friends.

Another trait children possess is the ability to openly express themselves verbally. They say what they feel without thinking twice about it. Some adults on the other hand find it difficult to express their feelings to others. This causes communication problems in close relationships. Whenever a person hurts our feelings and offends us, we are quick to hold grudges and develop revengeful attitudes toward them. Young children rarely dwell on past hurts or purposely act revengeful towards another.

Fear is a reaction that can mentally cripple a person and young children have no knowledge of it. It's impossible for them to conjure up bad thoughts about predicaments and work themselves into a frenzy like so many of us do. They are free of this unnecessary burden until fear becomes a learned behavior from parents, friends or television.

Another difference between adults and children is their innate sense to please their parents or people they love through their actions and achievements. Once adulthood is reached many of us tend to become selfish, without regard for anyone else's feelings about whether our actions or decisions hurt those we love.

So, try not to let your childlike qualities erode. Build on them and develop them. I remember playing mommy monster with my girls. I would place a sheet over my head and run around the house chasing them. I felt like a kid again and we all had fun. Being silly is a joyful pastime. Although my kids are adults now, they all have fond memories of this game we use to play.

Abandon yourself in creative, enjoyable pastimes with loved ones. It will definitely make you feel alive again.

Our Physical Body is an Extension of our Spiritual Being

We are all on a life-journey. As mentioned previously, unless we are living our lives in complete harmony with our spirit, this journey will never be experienced with complete peace and happiness. Many of us are stuck in bondage and we cannot experience the full joy that God desires us to experience. We are unhappy with our appearance, our jobs, our children and our relationships. We even find that our daily activities do not bring any satisfaction. We are in a limbo state of existence.

This state of just BEING is NOT what was intended for each of us. When we become stale with life, then life holds no value or meaning to us. That is why suicide has crept into the lives of so many people who have lost hope in themselves.

There is a higher power within each of us available to guide us along the pathways of life and create inner peace at all times. This higher power is the 'God' within us all. Self love is an important aspect of this higher power.

Many of us are unhappy with ourselves and we do not possess the ability or strength to stick to any plan of action that will create the new image or lifestyle we desire. We try many times, but set ourselves up for failure. Most of us start out with good intentions, but soon lose interest and become embarrassed by the 'enthusiasm' we once showed others about desiring to change our life.

When it comes to your physical or spiritual development - seek heavenly assistance; the most powerful assistance there is in the universe. Talk to God, your guardian angels, and deceased loved ones about your desire or need for change and your plan of action. They will give you the new found strength that no friend or loved one may be able to offer. Don't get me wrong - we all have good friends and bad ones. Just stay away from the ones who don't offer any compassion or positive input when you need it the most.

Accept, Accept, Accept

Acceptance of others for what they are and not who they can be or should be - is important as we travel along our spiritual path. All of us were born into different families with different backgrounds and learning experiences. These experiences stay with us for a lifetime. Some people lived with criticism so they easily find fault with others, some people were raised with abuse, so they learn to be distrustful. Whatever our background and learning experiences, sometimes it is best to look past other's faults and shortcomings and just LOVE.

One day while sitting in my car waiting for my five year olds' Kindergarten class to be dismissed, I saw a young toddler running a few steps behind her mother. Suddenly, she tumbled onto the concrete walkway and laid there crying. The mother bent down and pulled her back up on her feet. The young girl hurriedly flung her arms around her mother's neck as she bent down to console her.

Love heals us. Love comforts us. Love fills our hearts with joy. One of the definitions found in the dictionary for LOVE is "the brotherly concern for others." When love is given wholeheartedly toward others - it multiplies and returns to us in one way or another.

When you can sit back and love those around you, whether they act the same as you or feel the same as you about important matters, that is acceptance. Tolerance is the key word to advancement of your spiritual being.

Get Involved in Life Around You

It is our birthright to get involved and make a difference in people's lives. Although we are all on this earthly plane to learn a different spiritual lesson than anyone else, maybe a part of another's development and growth is to be influenced or inspired by you.

When my three daughters were young, I decided to get them involved in volunteer work. I planned for us to make weekly visits to a hospital where retired nuns lived. One floor of the hospital was dedicated to house the Sisters of Charity from Greensburg for two years while their new mother house was being built.

My daughter's began preparing for our first visit and painstakingly drew tons of pictures to take to the nuns so they would have colorful decorations to hang on their blank walls. I learned that this type of activity not only helped the nuns, but it helped my children's self-esteem as well. They soon began to feel comfortable with the visits and my youngest would dance for the nuns while her sister would play her portable piano or violin. They enjoyed the audience's happy reactions to their performances.

Getting involved in life doesn't necessarily mean taking on more charitable activities than you can handle. I was a soccer/basketball/track mom. I realize how life can be hectic for all of us. But sometimes being a silent healer and making yourself available for family and friends who are in need of support can also be a great way to make a difference in a person's life.

Spiritual profit comes easily to those who take time to get involved in the world around them. Also, we can make a difference in society by speaking up. Don't be a quiet bystander. If you see an injustice being done, speak up. If you see something that makes you feel uncomfortable or sad - do something. Sometimes it only takes speaking up to influence a person.

Someone reading this may know of a person who is abusive toward another, but they chose to sit back and be a bystander because they don't want to get involved. Someone reading this may know of a person who is contemplating suicide but they may chose to sit back and let the person deal with their depression on their own. Someone reading this may know of a person who is an alcoholic and drives while under the influence. They may feel best ignoring the situation, but this person is at risk every time they go out. They can easily kill themselves and other innocent people unless they get the help they need.

Remember - our involvement may be necessary in order to bring about a positive end result or to help others progress along their paths.

Our Power Within

Whenever I hear a person say, "If it's God's will it will happen," I feel uncomfortable. Why would anyone limit themselves to the God Power they possess inside. God is part of us and we are part of Him. He is not a far away entity or Being who leads us in every single decision and choice we make; remember we were given free will.

God didn't model us into human puppets whom he chooses to control whenever He desires. He molded us into His own image with His power inside of us to guide us, protect us and inspire us. This spark of God power is the best part of each of us and carries with it a lot of divinity and strength.

I'm not saying it's wrong to surrender a problem to God. In fact, I encourage it; especially if the problem is overwhelming. But to leave everything up in the air and just WAIT for God to bring you a new home or a loving mate or to wait for His will to take place - doesn't make sense to me.

It's God's will for us to believe in ourselves and our abilities by tapping into His power. In the New Testament it says, "The truth will set you free." If you were to look up the meaning of truth in the dictionary one of its meanings is simply "God." God will set us free. The God who rules from his most high and the God within our spirits - or other words our Christ consciousness.

Future Quests

I recently overheard some children discuss what they wanted to be when they grew up. I couldn't help but interject my own feelings to their conversation. "I'm still trying to figure out what I want to be when I grow up!" I said. Part of me was jeering of course, but part of me meant it. At the age of 60 I feel that I have accomplished a lot of good things in my life, but I still want to make the next twenty years count for myself. I raised three beautiful and successful daughters who spend much time with me and dote on me often.

I have self-published two children's books and two novels which are on sale on Amazon.com. I have written numerous articles and stories for local newspapers and magazines, but I desire to continue working on other writing projects to bring self-fulfillment.

My dreams have always been important to me, but I've realized that I really, really need to accomplish them in order to put the icing on the cake for me. In other words, I don't ever want to leave this world with any regrets of any kind! Life is not something that is to slip by. Life is something we are to endear and hold precious.

It would be wonderful to sit back in our old age and use these words to describe our past life - Dynamic, Fulfilling, Adventurous and FUN.

We are all born with a timetable to spend on earth, but many of us don't even consider this timetable, we tend to keep following unfulfilling schedules and remaining in unfulfilling relationships without thinking of how much time we have to accomplish our hearts desire until we are past middle age and sometimes by then, it may be too late.

The Company You Keep

I am a firm believer that a person should spend maximum time with people who make them feel completely comfortable with themselves and nourish and support who they are. Keeping company with these type of loving individuals will enhance your life.

Keeping company with individuals who tend to be negative and who complain about their life constantly can begin to physically affect you negatively. The stress that these type of people can cause you can make you sick and actually make you feel drained of energy.

I once knew a co-worker who had disagreements with one particular friend repeatedly. This co-worker was a very passive, accepting person who happened to find herself in a friendship with a person who picked her apart all the time and always criticized most things that she did. This would cause unnecessary arguments between them.

Evidently my co-worker's friend had a different concept of friendship and love between friends - and this got to the point that my co-worker couldn't stand to be around her negative friend any longer.

Friction should never be a part of ANY relationship. And if it is - take a hike far away from this person. This goes for any relationship. Being with a supportive, loving partner is of utmost importance. If you are unsure about a relationship, ask yourself this question - *If I had six months to live, would I want them to be spent with that person?* If your soul resonates a loud NO - then this is a truth that needs acted upon.

Our soul needs encouragement and love from others. You can decide whether to include another person in your life or not and it is not wrong to decide not to; especially if that person causes you to feel low self-esteem about yourself. I'm not saying that you should totally avoid being in the company of people who you feel are not as good as you are, that would be egotistical. Jesus himself spent time with criminals and prostitutes and didn't feel above them.

But sometimes people are on a different level of consciousness than you are (spiritually) and they will never view the world or people or circumstances the same way as you do. Choosing to limit your time around these type of people will help you to feel more balanced in life. It doesn't mean that you are acting unloving or not accepting others - it just means that you are making a decision to take more control of your life so you are more fulfilled.

Good Decision Making

The most difficult part of our daily existence is our decision making or the right to exercise our gift of free will. Each day we are called upon to make decisions, but many of us rarely contemplate making these decisions on a spiritual level which will cultivate our self-love and self-empowerment.

For instance, in the past there have been times when I acted improperly while upset with my children. I tended to yell loudly at them when I felt frustrated at their actions. It took a few times of hearing them remark, "You don't have to be so mean about it," that I realized I hadn't made the right choice in my actions toward them. My bad decision became a learning experience for me and I came to realize that we all have two choices in any given situation; the right choice or the wrong choice.

I once heard that nothing can be accomplished by force, only through co-operation. If our decision making were looked at from this point of view, I feel that we would consider all consequences of our behavior before acting inappropriately. Blaming others for your behavior is an example of making the wrong choice. So, the old adage, "She made me so upset" or "It's because of you that I acted that way" is really not the case. No one can MAKE a person do something or feel a certain way unless they make the decision to do so themselves. So bad actions, whether they are verbal or physical toward another is a self-induced choice and others should never be blamed for that choice or bad behavior.

It is really easy to decide what the correct decision should be in any given situation. Ask yourself, "If I act this way would it make this person feel better or worse?" If the answer is 'worse' than this decision may also affect your spirit in a negative manner and should be reconsidered.

Use Your Spiritual Vision Daily

If we took time to view our daily circumstances and experiences with spiritual awareness, we would be pleasantly surprised. Every incident whether it be an argument with a spouse or the receipt of a gift or a physical injury, happens for a reason.

We see people in the news daily experiencing tragedy and using the experience as a stepping stone to help others in their community. Many organizations and support groups would not have been created had it not been for a tragedy. Often times people need to have a voice or make a difference by their suffering by sharing their grief with others who may be experiencing the same type of pain.

By using your spiritual vision you will view people from all walks of life differently. I remember as a young teenager I judged people by their clothes, their cars, their home, etc. But now I see everyone on a spiritual level. I realize that they are doing the best that they know how and that they are here to live a life with lessons of their own to learn.

Our life is about SELF-DISCOVERY. The more we learn about our self and our reasoning behind our behavior - the more we progress on our life path.

Understanding our self is the key to success and how we relate to others and our decisions are an important factor in self-discovery.

If for some reason you make a bad decision in life - learn from it and move on. Use it as a cleansing experience because most of our mistakes are meant to happen to teach us something about ourselves or someone else.

The Importance of Explanations

Have you ever been real upset at another person or child? I'm sure the answer would be yes. But, during the course of your anger did you ever stop to ask for an explanation or reason for the person or child's behavior or attitude first?

Explanations open the door for negotiation and understanding. Most of the time explanations heal our pain and anger. Once we hear the reasoning behind another's actions, we can then say - THAT'S WHY. That's why they acted this way or that way. It sometimes doesn't excuse the pain another person caused, but it offers insights that assist in comprehending the situation.

Once while at a house party I witnessed the hostess kick a male guest out of her house. She totally flipped out and began to scream and swear at him when she found him alone with her four year old daughter. The two of them were sitting on the child's bedroom floor playing a board game. Since the bedroom was right beside the room where the party was being held and the door was wide open, the guests looked at each other in complete shock. They were embarrassed at how the mother acted publicly. I, on the other hand could understand her overactive behavior. The mother had been sexually molested for years at the hands of her father and his best friend when she was a young child. Because of this she had a difficult time trusting men.

There is always an explanation for other people's actions and remarks, and sometimes we will never know the truth of the matter. But, if you ever find yourself in an uncomfortable situation try asking the person WHY they made the remarks that hurt you - or WHY they treated you the way they did. This question will take them by surprise, but by giving them an opportunity to explain, both parties have an opportunity to heal and feel less burdened.

Hold Your Tongue

I'm sure that all of us have been in situations that warranted rude comments or inconsiderate back talk to others. But, how we respond to these incidents can either help us or hinder us in the development of our spirit.

For example, we have all witnessed scenes from talk shows whereby people have used ignorant and malicious comments toward one another. But, what good comes from this type of behavior? It surely doesn't make the person who directed the comments look like a decent, kind-hearted individual and it only embarrasses the person it was directed at.

Sowing love and respect at all times no matter what the situation is the only way to FEEL empowered and in control. Hold that tongue when faced with anger and replace it with love, the results will be unbelievable. It is easy to be spiteful and out of control, but it takes discipline to react lovingly.

When I was seventeen years old I happened to become involved with a person who was not the best choice for a boyfriend. We dated for three years and became engaged. One night my fiancée went out on the town, got drunk and ended up being unfaithful to me with a woman I happened to know. Being the type of person that I was at the time, I forgave the man and continued on with our relationship.

Months later we were to attend a wedding and the woman my fiancée had his affair with was to attend as well. I spent a lot of time and energy rehearsing the cruel words I was going to spew at her that night if we happened to cross paths and this caused me a lot of sleepness nights.

While at the wedding it was easy to stay clear of the other woman since it was a large crowd but at some point in time I went up to the bar to get a drink and suddenly the other woman was standing right beside me. Without thinking I turned to her and said hello.

She looked at me very surprised but began a nice conversation with me. I then surprised myself and stood there speaking with her in a friendly manner as well. I learned that she was a nicer person than my fiancée, and I ended up dumping him shortly thereafter.

Although I had intentions to tell this girl off, I'm glad I held my tongue and treated her with acceptance. What good would it have done anyway?

Everyone makes mistakes and gets themselves in situations that they later regret. I'm glad this episode occurred because it taught me an invaluable lesson. Sowing love and respect is the only way to FEEL empowered and in control. I'm not saying to take bad treatment from others. I feel it's of utmost importance to express your feelings to others, but in a civil manner. Hold that tongue when faced with anger and replace it with love - the results will be unbelievable.

I have always taught my children one thing - A PERSONS INTENTIONS MEAN THE MOST. If a person did not purposely set out to hurt you or cause you harm or pain, then why should they be treated badly over an incident with good intentions?

An easier example of this would be like a child spilling a glass of milk. They don't intentionally spill the milk, so why should anyone get upset over their actions?

Don't Limit Yourself

If I had one thing to stress to people today it would be - Don't Limit Yourself. When people feel that God is a far away entity and not an entity that is also present within themselves, they limit their life and tend to not experience success. When I say success, I do not mean it in the way many people view success. In the spiritual sense, success is not measured in how much money you make or how big of a house you live in, it's how you feel within yourself or how you perceive yourself.

A person can win the big lottery but still have nothing because they lack the sense of spiritual contentment or love of God through themselves. As mentioned earlier, we are all equipped with overwhelming God power, to assist us in accomplishing our goals and desires. We do not need to take a passive seat in life and just BE, we are bigger than ourselves.

While vacationing in Harrisburg my family and I visited some caverns. While exploring the caves with our guide he explained that a hermit had lived in the caverns for 19 years at one point in history and had written a manuscript about his life of solitude. After the hermit died, his booklet was published and was offered for sale in the souvenir shop. I purchased a copy and was amazed at its' wisdom. It was entitled, "The Sweets of Solitude, or Instructions to Mankind - How they May be Happy in a Miserable World." The hermit, Amos Wilson, stated, "My situation has no doubt been pronounced unhappy and miserable by many … but secluded as I have been from the society of man, depriving myself of the superfluities of life, I solemnly declare that I have enjoyed more real happiness than what all the riches of this world could have afforded me."

Although this hermit limited himself of worldly goods, he didn't limit himself to God Power, which enabled him to experience spiritual contentment while confined.

The End Result

I have come to gain a lot of wisdom throughout my sixty years. I have come to realize that life is never easy and our lives are similar to a roller coaster ride - full of ups and downs. But, as I have repeated over and over again in this book, if we possess spiritual contentment and spiritual understanding, the downs will become bearable for us.

Even in the happiest of lives, people will experience bouts of sadness and discontentment, but again - if our spiritual life is in order, we will possess the strength necessary to handle these emotions and the negativity of any situation will be short-lived.

I remember a conversation with one of my daughter's when she was very young. She asked, "God made us happy, why can't we stay that way?" I didn't truly know how to answer her properly because she had a point. But in thinking this through it only made sense to surmise that a person cannot develop and grow spiritually if they were not challenged.

In looking over my past life I began to notice some similarities in my experiences that presented the same type of challenges in my life. For example, I charted by life into four age groups. Age 0-10, age 10-20, age 20-30 and age 30-60. I logged as many life experiences I could recall (good and bad) and made notes of the emotions I felt about the experiences.

One experience occurred while I was in First Grade living on an Army base in Japan. I decided to walk home for lunch one day to surprise my mother. I never left the school grounds during lunch period before, but felt compelled to eat lunch at home for a change. After the school guard crossed me and the other school-age children across the street to the Army barracks, everyone dispersed and I was left alone to find my house. Suddenly all the houses looked the same and I couldn't seem to find my home among the rows and rows of duplexes.

I began to cry and I didn't know what to do with myself. I walked back and forth in a circle sobbing for what seemed to be an eternity. Suddenly, a woman appeared and asked my name. She happened to know my mother and took me to her home to call her. She fed me vegetable soup until my mother came to pick me up.

During this 'life episode' I experienced fear and loneliness (although it was short-lived), and also felt gratitude for the woman's kindness. Of course this was during the 1960's and I wasn't taught to fear strangers then.

In each age group of mine, I noticed that I experienced a lot of the same type of emotions on a recurring basis. Sadness, loneliness and rejection were present as well as love, happiness and success. Throughout our lifetime we all experience the same basic emotions, but different circumstances bring about these emotions.

When I was eight years old my younger sister, Shawn, was in the hospital awaiting open heart surgery. I remember asking my grandmother if my sister could die. She bluntly answered, "yes." I remember escaping to my bedroom and pleading with God all night for her well being. I experienced the fear of possibly losing someone I loved. I think all of us have experienced this emotion at one time or another during our life, and it's quite scary.

Try charting your life. I believe that on an emotional level there is a universal similarity between us all. The end result is, "We are meant to see the world universally through the same glasses as everyone else, but the world may seem more clearer to some than for others." When we are out of focus, it is sometimes difficult to understand the spiritual message our soul needs for growth or nourishment.

It is also during these 'out of focus' times that we NEED God and we turn to him for guidance and comfort. If our life experiences only warranted good emotions - we would never draw close to God and he would be forgotten.

Through negativity we are reminded of our need for Him in our life.

If you have experienced a miracle or angel encounter,
feel free to contact the author at the email address below:

Rorossey@gmail.com

Printed in Poland
by Amazon Fulfillment
Poland Sp. z o.o., Wrocław